YOUR KNOWLEDGE HAS VALUE

Sabrina Höling

Fertility Decline and Son Preference in India

Does fertility decline promote or hinder gender bias in mortality?

GRIN Verlag

Bibliografische Information der Deutschen Nationalbibliothek:

Die Deutsche Bibliothek verzeichnet diese Publikation in der Deutschen National-
bibliografie; detaillierte bibliografische Daten sind im Internet über http://dnb.d-
nb.de/ abrufbar.

Imprint:

Copyright © 2011 GRIN Verlag GmbH
Druck und Bindung: Books on Demand GmbH, Norderstedt Germany
ISBN: 978-3-656-44613-2

This book at GRIN:

http://www.grin.com/en/e-book/184321/fertility-decline-and-son-preference-in-
india

GRIN - Your knowledge has value

Der GRIN Verlag publiziert seit 1998 wissenschaftliche Arbeiten von Studenten, Hochschullehrern und anderen Akademikern als eBook und gedrucktes Buch. Die Verlagswebsite www.grin.com ist die ideale Plattform zur Veröffentlichung von Hausarbeiten, Abschlussarbeiten, wissenschaftlichen Aufsätzen, Dissertationen und Fachbüchern.

Visit us on the internet:

http://www.grin.com/

http://www.facebook.com/grincom

http://www.twitter.com/grin_com

Georg-August-Universität-Göttingen

Wintersemester 2011/2012

Seminar: Gender based Violance: Missing Women, Human Trafficking and Domestic and

Sexual Violance

Submitted on 29th of November 2011

Fertility Decline and Son Preference in India

Does fertility decline in India promote or hinder gender bias in mortality?

Sabrina Franziska Höling

BA Economics/Political Science

5. Semester

Abstract

In the backdrop of the debate on missing women and son preference in Asia, this paper deals with the influence of fertility decline in India on gender bias in mortality. In order to get more precise answers, the text concentrates on gender bias in pre- natal mortality and infant mortality. I will test two contradicting hypotheses empirically using among others data from three rounds of the National Family Health Survey in India (1992, 1998 and 2005). These constitute the foundation for further studies in order to answer the question whether fertility decline promotes or hinders gender bias in mortality. Judging the relation of these two variables by female education will show the strong link between female education and fertility. I will find out that son preference in India stays constant, independent from the mother´s educational level. Nonetheless, this text will show that the level of female education determines how parents interfere with their child´s sex. Empirical data will prove that higher educated women prefer pre-natal technology for girl elimination while uneducated women have less access to or knowledge of it. The data will also suggest that less educated mothers have a higher daughter infanticide rate. I will conclude that fertility decline intensifies gender bias in pre- natal mortality. However, the influence it might have on female infant mortality can not be estimated correctly because of incomplete empirical data.

Table of Contents

			Page
1.	List of abbreviations		5
2.	Introduction		5
3.	Fertility		6
	3.1.	Definition of Fertility	6
	3.2.	Fertility Decline in India	6
4.	Genders bias and Mortality		7
	4.1.	Origin of and Reasons for Gender Bias	7
	4.2.	Data of Gender Bias	7
	4.3.	Pre- natal Gender Bias: Abortion in India	8
	4.4.	Post- natal Gender Bias: Gender Bias in Child Mortality	9
5.	Contradicting Hypotheses		10
	5.1.	Hypotheses 1: Fertility Decline hinders Gender Bias in Mortality	11
	5.2.	Hypotheses 2: Fertility Decline promotes Gender Bias in Mortality	12
6.	Empirical Evidence to the Hypotheses: Fertility Decline intensifies Gender Bias in Mortality		13
7.	Conclusion		15
8.	References		17
	8.1.	Internet Recources	17
	8.2.	Monographs and Working Papers	17
9.	List of Figures		18
	9.1.	Figure 1: Child sex ratio 0-6 years and overall sex ratio, India 1961- 2011	18
	9.2.	Figure 2: Sex Ratio (girls per 1000 boys) of second order births by mother´s level of education	19

9.3. Figure 3: Infant mortality rate by mother´s education level,   20
      India 1992-1993

10. List of Tables   21
    10.1.   Table 1: National Family Health Survey (1-3)   21
    10.2.   Table 2: Sex ratio of total population and child population in the   22
       age group 0-6, India 1961- 2011

1. List of abbreviations

IMR   Infant mortality rate

NFHS   National Family Heath Survey in India

SRB   Sex ratio at birth

TFR   Total fertility rate

2. Introduction

Nobel prize winner Amartya Sen was one of the first scientists who explored female discrimination in Asia. Among other things, he examined gender inequality in mortality and natality. Over the last thirty years, several scientists followed Sen and conducted research to find the exact link between gender bias in mortality and fertility. India is an especially popular subject for studies because the country is known for a distinct female discrimination and a rising population.

Although, India´s population is today considered to be the second largest population in the world, India´s cencus in 2001 reported a steady fertility decline. At the same time, India´s female to male ratio shows a clear disadvantage of girls. Studies show a steadily declining fertility per women. Whereas, in general, the sex ratio is declining slowly, it is simultaneously rising among children. How are these two variables, fertility and female discrimination, connected? Furthermore, what influence might fertility decline have on gender bias in mortality? Are girls eliminated in favour of boys?

This paper will discuss the relationship between fertility decline and gender bias in mortality. This is a current issue because nobody is able to forsee what impact the missing women might have on India´s future. It is therefore necessary to explore the variables that are connected to gender bias in mortality.

 In the following, I limit the term "mortality" to pre-natal and infant mortality because this parameter leads to more significant and precise answers. In other words, I will deal with female fetus and infant mortality as a result of gender bias. In addition, I decided to take female education as a third variable into account. Firstly, in order to reduce the variablity of the result and secondly, because according to literature[1], female education has a significant independent relation to fertility and to gender bias in mortality. Therefore, one can assume that the use of female education as an endogenous variable could provide information about the influence fertility decline has on female deficit. Accordingly, fertility and gender bias in mortality are

---

[1] See References in the appendix

specified as exogenous variables. Since the term "fertility" is defined differently by various authors, this paper will start with a definition of the term. Then, it will concentrate on the presence of female discrimination and female deficit in India. Later, two hypotheses will be presented which give two contradicting possible answers to the question whether fertility decline promotes or hinders gender bias in mortality. In the end, empirical data from several sources like the Indian census of 2001, or the Family Health Surves will support one hypotheses and negate the other.

3. Fertility

3.1. Definition of Fertility

Women´s fertility is estimated by the total fertility rate (TFR). The TFR "represents the number of children that would be born to a woman if she lived to the end of her childbearing years and bore children at each age, in accordance with the prevailing age- specific fertility rates" (Murthi, Guiou, Drèze, 1995, p. 757). Moreover, scientific literature use the term TFR as an expanded measure for the birth rate because it is "independent of the age structure of the population" (Murthi, Guio, Drèze, 1995, p.757). In the following text, this interpretation of the term fertility will be used.

3.2. Fertility Decline in India

Over the last decades, fertility decline in India has been reported. According to the first National Family Health Survey (NFHS) of 1992/ 1993, the average total fertility rate per women was 3.4 children. In the next two surveys, NFHS-2 (1998-1999) and NFHS-3 (2005-2006) the TFR per women dropped first to 2.9 and then to 2.7 children. In addition, the percentage of women using any contraceptive method rose significantly from 40.7 in NFHS-1 to 48.2 in NFHS-2 and to 56.3 in NFHS-3[2]. The reduced desired family size was estimated by the fact that during the first survey 59.7 % percent of the questioned women claimed to not want any more children after having given births to two living children. In the second survey this percentag rose to 72.4 % and in the last survey even to 84.6%[3].

---

[2] It must be noted that, curiously, the highest percentage of women using contraceptives are women with an education under five years. This will be neglected in the following because no possible interpretation of this fact is known . However it is a fact, that women with education use more contraceptives than the one without any education.
[3] See Table 1

4. Gender Bias and Mortality

4.1. Origin of and Reasons for Gender Bias

In Indian society son preference is still strong. But where does it come from? For centuries, sons have been regarded as heirs, as the ones who sire the next generation and carry on the family name. Furthermore, sons usually inherit property because daughters are married into another family. In addition, sons represent security for their parents in old- age because they are obliged to take care of them. To clarify, sons are a status symbol and important for the family honor. In contrast, daughters have to be married off with the additional burdensome payment of a dowry to the husband´s family. According to Guilmoto (2007) "dowry encompasses cash, gold and other Jewellery [..] and it constitutes the major bulk of marriage expenses, often exceeding several years' of household income" (p.22). While it probably costs the same amount of money to raise a son or a daughter, sons are seen as an economic burden in the short run and in the long run as a guarantee for security. Women may cost as much as boys during the childhood (maybe even less due to more limited access to education etc.) but it will be more expensive to marry them off. But how is the situation in modern India today? How is gender bias present? The best way to analyze gender bias is by examining the sex ratio and actions like sex- selective abortion or female infanticide that promote son preference and girl elimination.

4.2. Data of Gender Bias

A method to estimate son preference is the sex ratio. With reference to the studies from the United Nations Secretariat of 1998, a "normal" sex ratio at birth lies between 103 to 106 males per 100 females (Arnold and Kishor, 2002). These numbers are a result of the scientific explanation that "as a matter of biology, the number of boys born is somewhat higher than the numbers of girls born" (Arnold and Kishor, 2002, p. 764). Due to this statistic, a higher sex ratio than 106 implies a higher girl discrimination because parents are successful in "avoiding the birth of a girl while insuring the birth of a boy" (Arnold, Kishor and Roy, 2002, p. 766). In fact, the sex ratio at birth in India was 105.1 during the NFHS-1 and 106.9 at the time of NFHS-2. Along with the Indian Cenus of 2001, the sex ratio for the under-six year old children was 107.8 males to 100 females or in other words 927 girls to 1000 boys[4] . These numbers show a significant rise in the sex ratio since comparatively in 1991 the number was lower with 105.8 boys to 100 girls. Equally important is to know that in some Indian states the sex ratio exceed

---

[4] See Table 2 and Figure 2

these numbers by a large margin. For instance in Punjyb, the sex ratio in 2001 was estimated as 126.1 (Arnold, Kishor and Roy, 2002 p.764).

In short, with reference to the United Nations Secretariat results, India´s high sex ratio, especially among the children under the age of six years, is a significant sign for gender bias. But how is gender bias in India pursued?

4.3. Pre-Natal Gender Bias: Abortion in India

To begin with, one explanation for the increasing sex ratio over the last decades is pre-natal technology, namely ultrasound and amniosentesis for sex determination and abortion for sex-selective elimination of fetuses. With the advent of amniosentesis in the 1970s, sex-determination in India became possible. Originally, the technology was intended to discover genetic abnormalities but eventually was used to determine the sex of the foetus. In 1976, the use of technology for foetal determination was prohibited. In 1994 the Indian government then tightened the law by a ban of sex-selective abortion in order to deal with the increasing number of sex-selective abortion[5]. Nontheless, the sex ratio worsened, and it is obvious that the law is nonexistant in practice (Arnold, Kisor and Roy, 2002). Government statistics from 1996 estimated that 0.6 million legal abortions are performed every year (Ministry of Health and Family Welfare, 1996).

Curiously it should be noted that there is a high probability that the number of abortions is underestimated since some induced abortions might be reported as spontaneous. In addition, the number of illegal abortions is assumed to be eight to eleven times higher than the number of legal ones (Arnold, Kishor, Roy, 2002, p. 761). And yet, one has to keep in mind that "having an abortion [...] does not in itself imply the use of technology for sex- selection" (Arnold, Kishor and Roy, 2002, p. 760). There are two possible reasons for women to have an abortion. First, they use abortion as a method of family planning because the family is not able to afford the child, because the woman´s health is at risk, or because the pregnancy is unwanted. Indeed, pre-natal technology could have found out that the fetus itself was not healthy and abortion can be used to save the family from the burden of a handicapped child. Second, abortion is used by couples to fulfill their desire to have a male child. In this case, parents use sex-determination tests and, according to the result, abort the unwanted female fetus. To demonstrate the second possible explanation, Arnold, Kishor and Roy discovered in their research in 2002 that "the sex ratio at birth is much higher if the mother had ultrasound and is even higher if the mother had

---

[5] Pre-Natal Diagnostic Techniques (Regulation and Prevention of Misuse) Act 1994

amniocentesis" (p. 775). Furthermore, research has shown, that one of six abortions was performed as the consequence of a sex- determination test (Arnold, Kishor and Roy, 2002).

To conclude, the advent of sex-determination technology and the better availability of abortion techniques led to a rise in the use of both. Nonetheless, son preference is only one reason to perform an abortion. Mainly, unwanted or unplanned pregnancies (independent from the sex of the fetus) have been reported as the reason. Even though, the officially reported explanation could hide the fact that sex-selection was the main reason, since the legal framework for an abortion is strict.

4.4. Post- natal Gender Bias: Child Mortality

SRB and abortion rates do not show the elimination of unwanted girls in its full extent. As a matter of fact, sex selection can be pursued after birth as well. It involves a passive strategy with the intention to give girls a lower survival chance than boys by witholding them from access to resources (Guilmoto, 2007). This type of female discrimination is extremely subtle and researchers are unable to explore their impact in its full dimension.

One way to examine the post-natal gender bias is to look at the infant mortality rate (IMR). Studies in developed countries have shown that, on average, the male infant mortality is higher than female IMR (Waldron 1983; Johansson and Nygren, 1991). Consequently, if the female IMR is higher than the male one, this will be considered to be an evidence for post- birth female deficit and son preference (Srinivasan and Bedi, 2006). India´s IMR in 2011 was estimated to be 47.57 deaths per 1000 live births but it has declined significantly over the years. Moreover, the male IMR was 46.18 deaths per 1000 male live births while the female IMR was 49.14 deaths per 1000 live births (Central Intelligence of the US). Again, it is very likely that the numbers are not accurate but underreported since parents will more likely report the death of a son if he dies at a young age than the death of a daughter (Das Gubta, Chung, Shouzhou, 2009, p.405).

However, the female mortality rate above the age of fifteen has continually improved over the years. Today, it is lower than the mortality rate of males over 25 years (Klasen and Wink, 2002). Obviously, gender bias affects the life expectancy of girls under the age of 6 more than older ones. With reference to the studies of Das Gubta, Chung and Shouzhou in 2009, the sex ratio of child mortality in India is the highest of children under the age of one and declines between the age of one and four years (see Table 1 p.404). This result can be taken as an evidence for female "infanticide and neglect" (Srinivasan and Bedi, 2006, p. 968). In the same way, one has to look at the variables that might influence the survival of females. These are namely the unequal

- 9 -

access to health care (post-natal care, immunization) and nutrition (quantity and quality). Both variables have effects on female IMR but the impact of less nutrition has been proven to be minor (Somerfelt and Arnoldt, 1999; Sen and Sengubta, 1993). Conversely, unequal access to health care for girls and boys leads to a higher mortality of young girls (Croll, 2001). Undoubtly, this gives evidence to the continuing son preference in India.

Therefore, it may be concluded that post-natal gender bias through "neglect is typically a low-tech technique [...] that requires almost no financial or other parental effort" (Guilmoto, 2007, p. 18).

5. Contradicting Hypotheses

As stated in the introduction, I will analyze the influence of fertility decline on gender bias in mortality by examining female education in India[6]. Firstly because all the variables named above have shown a significant change over the last decade. And secondly, female education seems to have an independent relation to fertility decline, son preference and both female pre-natal and infant mortality, as one can see in the graphic below.

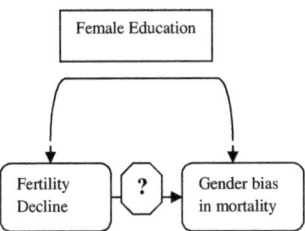

How could female education be related to these variables and set up an all inclusive relationship? In the following, I take female education as the endogenous variable and fertility decline and female mortality as the two exogenous variables. Additionally, we assume that fertilty decline has an influence on female pre- natal and infant mortality.

---

[6] There are various other factors like househould income, male education and female labor force participation that are not discussed here.

5.1. Hypothesis 1: Fertility Decline hinders Gender Bias in Mortality

Model 1:Fertility decline hinders gender bias in mortality

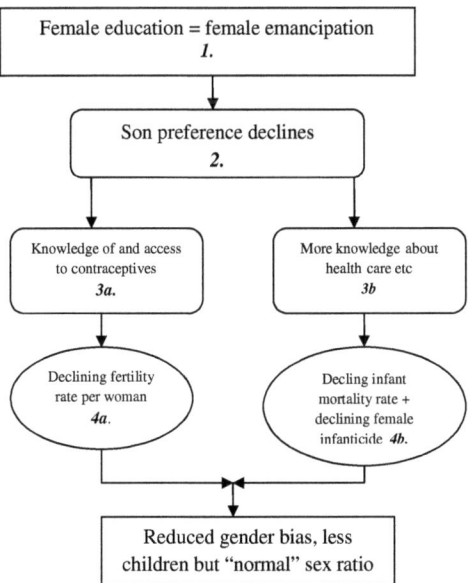

In theory, one could assume that higher female education would lead to more female emancipation because women are not reduced to their reproductive ability anymore (*1.*). These hypotheses allege a change in the Indian society towards gender equality, caused by a rise in female education. One could even go further and assume that the better women´s education is and the more she is emancipated, the less she depends on her sons for social status and security in later life. Accordingly, the son preference would diminish (*2.*). Additionally, educated women have more knowledge of, and more access to, contraceptives (*3a.*). They are able to plan the number of children they would like to have and don´t have to suffer from several unplanned or unwanted pregnancies. Furthermore, due to their higher level of education, they will probably marry later and start to have children at an older age. As a result, the fertility rate of higher educated women should be lower than the one of their less educated female counterparts (*4a.*). One could expect that female education results in a decline of the infant mortality rate as well because these women know more about health care and hygiene (*3b*) and therefore, improve the survival chances of their children (*4b.*). Moreover, they plan the number of children for which

they can provide nutrition, health care, etc. Without a doubt, female infant mortality rate (caused by gender bias) and the number of sex- selective abortions would be reduced.

As stated in this hypothesis, fertility decline caused by higher female education hinders gender bias in pre- and post-natal mortality. Unfortunately, there is no empirical data to prove the previously stated assumptions. In order to examine hypotheses 1, more fundamental research on the mechanisms that led to a rise or decline of son preference in India is necessary. Furthermore, it is not clear how female emancipation influences son preference. So far, no correlation between female education, emancipation and son preference can be verified

5.2. Hypothesis 2: Fertility Decline promotes Gender Bias in Mortality

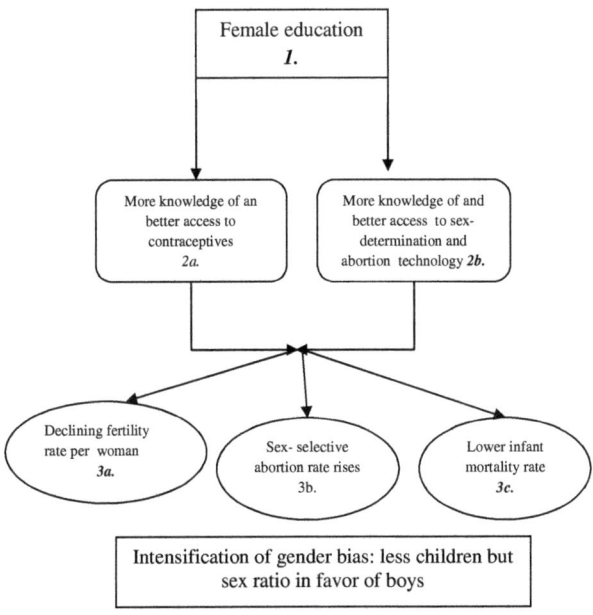

The reverse hypotheses is that the more highly educated a women is and the more she has knowledge of and access to contraceptives (**2a.**) and technology, like sex determination technology or abortion (**2b**), the more she will use it to go first, after her desired number of children, and second, after the desired sex of her child. In other words, this hypotheses is based on the assumption that rising female education does not change Indian society and does not improve gender equality. In this case, better education does not imply emancipation but merely

more possibilites to follow the traditional son preference. However, a higher education results in a declining fertility (*3a.*) and in a declining infant mortality rate in general[7] (*3c.*). Nontheless, as said before, son preference stays constant and therefore, gender bias is now expressed in female fetus´ abortions. In short, the female IMR might be lower because of the mother´s better knowledge of and the use of health care but the sex- selective abortion rate compensate this by rising in approximately the same extent (*3b.*). Hence, better education and a lower fertility rate intensify gender bias in pre-natal mortality.

Although, both hypotheses have their fundamental principles, the second one can be proven with empirical evidence. The following part will demonstrate that fertility decline promotes gender bias in pre-natal mortality and reduces post-natal female mortality if the relation is examined under the view of the female educational level.

6. Empirical Evidence to the Hypotheses: Fertility Decline intensifies Gender Bias in Mortality

To begin with, one has to examine the link between female education and each variable, and in a second step, look at the influence fertility decline might have on gender bias in mortality.

First, education in fact influences female fertility to a great extent. The NFHS- 3 [8] distinguishes between four levels of female education. The lowest level consists of women with no education at all (group 1). These women have a total fertility rate (TFR) of 3.6 children per woman. The TFR then declines with the increasing female education level. Women with an education under 5 years (group 2) have a TFR of 2.5, a five to nine years educated woman (group 3) has a TFR of 2.4 while the highest educated group of women (ten years and above) (group 4) have the lowest TFR estimated by 1.9 children per woman.

Furthermore, the female´s educational level provides information about her use of contraceptives. As a matter of fact, the higher educated a woman is, the more likely she is to use any contraceptive method. 52.1 percent of group 1 use any contraceptive method, while the number rises with the educational level to 61.1 percent of group 4. This proves that the theoretical assumptions made above are, so far, correct. Female education influences the use of contraceptives and fertility. Group 4 has the highest quota in contraceptive use and the lowest fertility rate. In conclusion, this can be seen as evidence to the fact, that fertility falls with a greater use of contraceptives which is a result of better female education.

---

[7] Here are the same reasons applicable as for the first theory above.
[8] See Table 1

But what about the sex ratio at birth? Here, the birth order has to be taken into account. According to studies by Arnold, Kishor and Roy in 2002, sex- selective interference in first pregnancies is not very common. However, the sex of the firstborn decides whether the parents will use sex- determination, sex- selective abortion or female infanticide at all to fullfill their desired number of sons. If the firstborn is male, researchers have found no suggestive decrease in the sex ratio for second order births (Jha, Bassani, 2011). But, if the firstborn is a girl, parents will more likely interfere during the second pregnancy. When one attributes this to a steady son preference, this can be a result of falling fertility. Parents want to make sure that, although, the number of children on the whole is reduced, the number of sons stays the same. This is verified by the fact that the sex ratio for second and third order births is higher than for the first (Arnold, Kishor, Roy, 2002). In addition, the sex ratio for the second and third child is worse among women with an education of ten years or above than among women with no education. The study of Jha in 2011[9] indicates that although, the sex ratio of second and third born children of group 1 mothers is higher than the natural sex ratio[10] (since it reaches its maximum in 2003 when the sex ratio was approximately 840 girls to 1000 boys), it is a lot lower than the SRB of children with mothers who belong to group 4. Their highest sex ratio over the decades is estimated by approximately 700 girls per 1000 boy in 2001.

Consequently, the better educated a woman is, the lower is the number of second born girls to boys. The significant difference of the SRB between the two levels of female education is an evidence for the more fruitful approach of educated women in their son preference through a more common use of sex- selective abortion. It confirms the theory above, that better education is a sign for more knowledge of and access to sex- determination and abortion technology.

The intermediate result is that female education has an influence on fertlity, contraceptives use and sex- selective abortion. In addition, so far it can be estimated that declining fertility promotes gender bias in pre- natal mortality.

The hypothesis that female education has an impact in infant mortality is true, as well[11]. The highest level of child mortality in general (100 deaths per 1000 live births) occur with uneducated (group 1) mothers. Mothers who belong to group 4 show the lowest level of IMR

---

[9] See Figure 2

[10] Remember: The natural sex ratio is between 950 to 975 girls per 1000 boys

[11] See Figure 3

(under 40 deaths per 1000 live births)[12]. Furthermore, statistics by Murthi, Guio and Dréze (1995) show that female literacy has not only a negative effect on IMR but in general it has an even larger effect on female infant mortality. Their statistics conclude that higher female education "reduces child mortality and anti-female bias in child survival" (Murthi, Guio, Drèze, 1995, p.764).

To sum up, lower educated mothers seem to neglect their daughters rather after the birth as an expression of their son preference, while high educated women use sex- selective abortion in order to have the desired number of sons. Additionally, a higher fertility decline leads to a higher sex- ratio at birth. Consequently, if parents can influence their child's sex, they don't have to use "a low- tech technique" (Guilomoto, 2007, p.18) like girl infanticide to eliminate unwanted daughters.

In other words, fertility decline promotes gender bias in pre-natal mortaliy through sex- selective abortion and reduces gender bias in post-natal mortality.

7. Conclusion

In conclusion, the above data demonstrates that fertility and female education are negatively related. Therefore, fertility decline and its impact on gender bias in mortality cannot be estimated without female education being taken into account. Furthermore, the relation between fertility decline and gender bias in mortality is proven. However, the exact correlation is still unclear. Following the hypothetical approach from above and using female education as the endogenous variable, the empirical data supports the assumption, that a declining fertility leads to an intensified gender bias in pre-natal (through sex- determination technology and abortion methods) mortality.

The prospect of having less children per women does not influence the desired number of sons. Parents still wish to have two, or at least one son. A lower total fertility rate per woman, caused, for example, by a higher use of contraceptives, or a reduced desired family size, reduces the chances of having a son. Therefore, the tendency exists for parents to interfere in order to have an influence on their child's sex. The significant rise in the sex-ratio of second born children demonstrates this fact. Through sex determination, in the early stages of the pregnancy, and the use of sex-selective abortion, couples are able to interfere. While this might be true, the official number of sex determination and sex-selective abortions are probably underreported because

---

[12] See Figure 3

both is prohibited by law. Consequently, the exact impact of fertility decline on gender bias in pre-natal mortality is still unknown.

Lower educated women, who have a higher TFR, might have a higher female infant mortality rate, but it is unclear if this can be taken as evidence for female infanticide as a result of declining fertility. Moreover, more data on female infant mortality and female infanticide needs to be collected. To estimate the impact fertility decline might have on female infanticide, one has to examine the influence other variables might have, e.g. urbanization, access to health care or household income. Female education as the only variable is not enough to determine the exact consequences.

To sum up, fertility decline intensifies gender bias in pre-natal female mortality. However, the studies are far from being complete and the underreported numbers in India hinder a correct collection and interpretation of the empirical data. Therefore, the low representativity of the empirical data above must be noted. Moreover, no measure has been found to calculate son preference so far. Hypothesis 1 could not be verified because there is no causality between female education, emancipation and son preference. Even in a developing India, son preference stays the same. Therefore, further studies have to be performed in order to find the mechanism which influence son preference.

8. References

8.1. Internet Recources

The world Factbook by the Central Intelligence Agency of the US
https://www.cia.gov/library/publications/the-world-factbook/rankorder/2091rank.html
pageview: 11/11/2011

Ministry of Health and Welfare, Government of India
http://mohfw.nic.in/ , pageview: 11/10/2011

Gender Composition of the Population in India from the Indian Cencus 2001
http://www.censusindia.net/ 11/11/2011

8.2. Monographs and Working Papers

Arnold, F./ Kishor, S./ Roy, T.K., (2002), Sex- Selective Abortion in India, in: Population and Development Review, Vol. 28, No. 4. pp. 759- 785

Croll, E., (2001), Endangered daughters: Discrimination and Development in Asia, London: Routledge

Das Gubta, M./ Chung, W./Shouzhou, L., (2009), Evidence for an Incipient Decline in Numbers of Missing Girls in China and India, in: Population and Development Review, Vol. 35, No. 4, pp. 401- 416

Guilmoto, Christophe Z., (2007), Characteristics of Sex- Ratio Imbalance in India, and Future Scenarios, in: the Journal of the United Nation Population Fund at the 4th Asia Conference on Reproductive and Sexual Healths and Rights October 29-31, 2007, Hyderabad (India)

Johansson, S/Nygren, O., (1991), The missing girls of China: a new demographic account, in: Population and Development Review, Vol. 17, No. 1, pp. 35- 51

Klasen, S./ Wink, (2002), A Turning Point in Gender Bias in Mortality? An update on the Number of Missing Women, in: Population and Development Review, Vol. 28, No. 2, pp. 285- 312

Murthi,M./ Guio, A.-C./ Drèze, J., (1995), Mortality, Fertility and Gender- Bias in India: A Distict- Level Analysis, in: Population and Devolpment Review, Vol. 21, No. 4, pp. 745- 782.

Prabhat Jha, Maya A Kesler, Rajesh Kumar, Faujdar Ram, Usha Ram, Lukasz Aleksandrowicz, Diego G Bassani, Shailaja Chandra, Jayant K Banthia (2011), Trends in selective abortions of girls in India: analysis of nationally representative birth histories from 1990 to 2005, in The Lancet, Vol. 377, pp 1921- 1928

Sen, A./ Sengubta, S., (1983), Maltnutrition of rural children and the sex bias, in: Economic and Political Weekly, Vol. 18, pp. 866- 864

Somerfelt, E./ Arnoldt, F., (1999), Sex differentials in the nutritional status of young children, in: United Nation (ed), Too young to Die: Genes or Gender?, New York: United Nations

Srinivasan, S./ Bedi, A.S., (2006), Daughter Elimination in Tamil Nadu, India: A Tale of Two Ratios, in: Journal of Development Studies, Vol. 44, No. 7, pp. 961- 990

Waldron, I., (1983), Sex Diferences in Human Mortality: The Role of Genetic Factors, in: Social Science and Medicine, Vol. 17, No. 6, pp. 321- 333

9. List of Figures

9.1. Figure 1:

Child sex ratio 0-6 years and overall sex ratio, India: 1961-2011

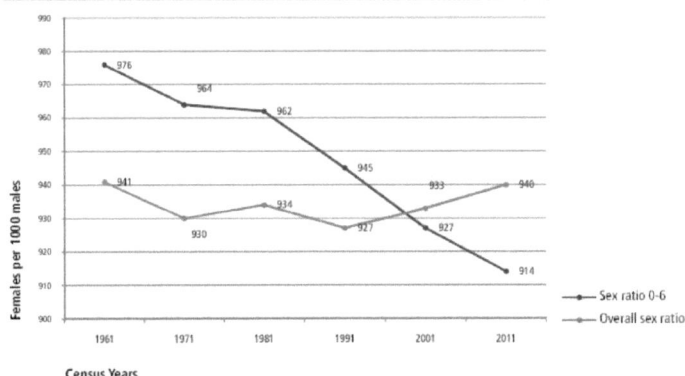

Source: Gender Composition of the Population, Census 2011, published on www.educationforallindia.com

9.2. Figure 2: Sex Ratio (girls per 1000 boys) of second order births by mother´s level of education

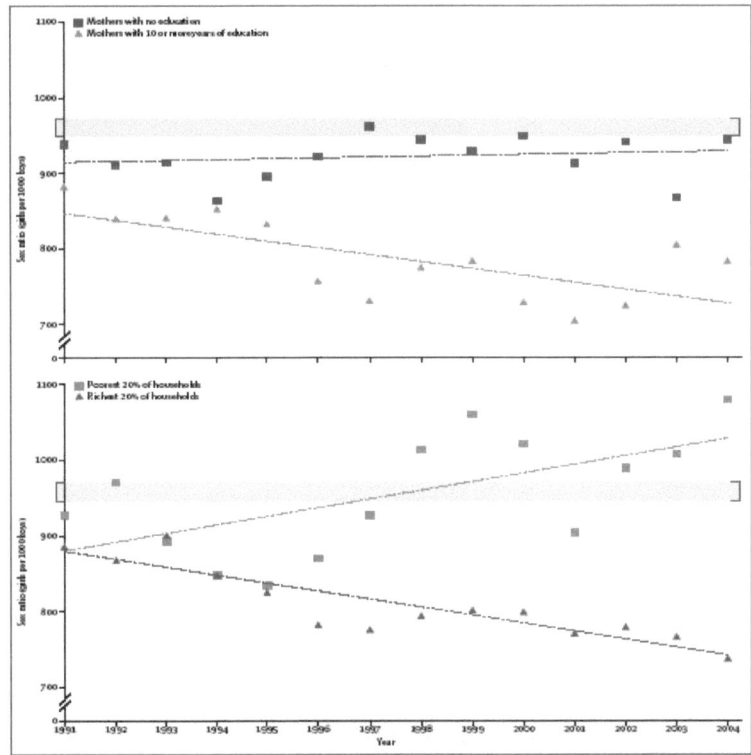

Figure 2: Sex ratio (girls per 1000 boys) of second-order births, if firstborn was a girl, by mother's level of education and household wealth index, from 1990–2005. Red brackets show the natural sex ratio range of 950–975 girls per 1000 boys. Test for trend: illiterate, p=0.347; grade 10 or higher, p=0.014; poorest 20%, p=0.026; richest 20%, p=0.002.

Prabhat Jha, Maya A Kesler, Rajesh Kumar, Faujdar Ram, Usha Ram, Lukasz Aleksandrowicz, Diego G Bassani, Shailaja Chandra, Jayant K Banthia (2011), Trends in selective abortions of girls in India: analysis of nationally representative birth histories from 1990 to 2005, in: The Lancet, Vol. 377, p. 1924

9.3. Figure 3: Infant mortality rate by mother´s education level, India (1992-1993)

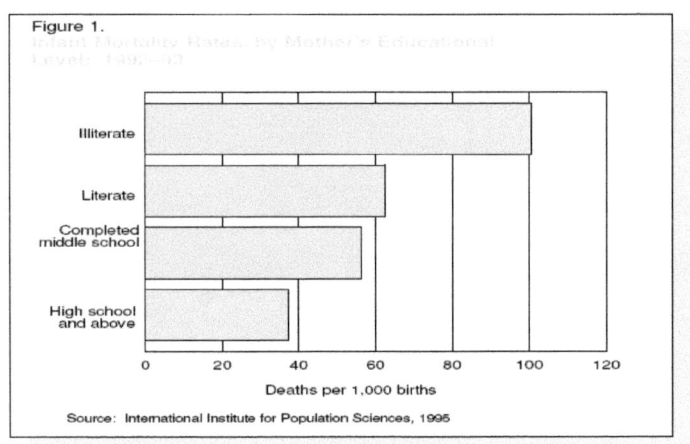

Figure 1.

Source: Velkoff, V.A, (1998), Women´s Education in India, U.S. Department of Commerce, p.1

10. List of Tables 10.1. Table 1: National Family Health Survey

Key Indicators for India from NFHS-3	NFHS-3 (2005-06)	Residence		Education				NFHS-2 (1998-99)	NFHS-1 (1992-93)
		Urban	Rural	No education[4]	<5 years complete[4]	5-9 years complete[4]	10 years complete and above[4]		
Marriage and Fertility									
1. Women age 20-24 married by age 18 (%)	47.4	29.3	56.2	76.5	64.8	46.2	14.1	50.0	54.2
2. Men age 25-29 married by age 21 (%)	32.3	18.1	40.3	56.4	46.8	34.0	16.4	na	na
3. Total fertility rate (children per woman)	2.7	2.1	3.0	3.6	2.5	2.4	1.9	2.9	3.4
4. Women age 15-19 who were already mothers or pregnant at the time of the survey (%)	16.0	8.7	19.1	32.6	21.2	13.5	5.2	na	na
5. Median age at first birth for women age 25-49	19.8	20.9	19.3	18.7	19.0	20.1	23.6	19.3	19.4
6. Married women with 2 living children wanting no more children[1] (%)	84.6	89.7	81.6	75.7	87.0	86.8	92.1	72.4	59.7
6a. Two sons	89.9	92.1	88.6	83.5	91.7	92.4	95.0	82.7	71.5
6b. One son, one daughter	87.0	92.8	85.3	79.0	91.2	90.4	94.7	76.4	66.0
6c. Two daughters	61.4	74.7	54.4	48.0	62.0	63.5	77.5	47.0	36.9
Family Planning (currently married women, age 15-49)									
Current use									
7. Any method (%)	56.3	64.0	53.0	52.1	63.0	58.6	61.1	48.2	40.7
8. Any modern method (%)	48.5	55.8	45.3	45.7	55.5	50.2	50.4	42.8	36.5
8a. Female sterilization (%)	37.3	37.8	37.1	39.7	46.7	37.8	26.0	34.1	27.4
8b. Male sterilization (%)	1.0	1.1	1.0	1.2	1.4	0.8	0.9	1.9	3.5
8c. IUD (%)	1.7	3.2	1.1	0.6	0.7	1.9	5.2	1.6	1.9
8d. Pill (%)	3.1	3.8	2.8	1.8	3.9	4.5	4.0	2.1	1.2
8e. Condom (%)	5.2	9.8	3.2	2.2	2.7	5.3	14.7	3.1	2.4
Unmet need for family planning									
9. Total unmet need (%)	12.8	9.7	14.1	13.6	10.4	12.9	11.4	15.8	19.5
9a. For spacing (%)	6.2	4.5	6.9	5.5	5.2	7.4	6.5	8.3	11.0
9b. For limiting (%)	6.6	5.2	7.2	8.1	5.2	5.5	4.9	7.5	8.5
Maternal and Child Health									
Maternity care (for births in the last 3 years)									
10. Mothers who had at least 3 antenatal care visits for their last birth (%)	50.7	73.8	42.8	29.8	52.1	64.6	85.3	44.2	43.9
11. Mothers who consumed IFA for 90 days or more when they were pregnant with their last child (%)	22.3	34.5	18.1	9.5	20.6	27.5	49.4	na	na
12. Births assisted by a doctor/nurse/LHV/ANM/other health personnel (%)[2]	48.8	75.3	39.9	27.9	48.0	61.9	86.8	42.4	33.0
13. Institutional births (%)[2]	40.8	69.4	31.1	19.8	38.9	52.9	80.6	33.6	26.1
14. Mothers who received postnatal care from a doctor/nurse/LHV/ANM/other health personnel within 2 days of delivery for their last birth (%)[2]	36.8	60.8	28.5	18.0	34.1	46.4	73.4	na	na
Child immunization and vitamin A supplementation[3]									
15a. Children 12-23 months fully immunized (BCG, measles, and 3 doses each of polio/DPT) (%)	43.5	57.6	38.6	26.1	46.1	55.3	71.0	42.0	35.5
15b. Children 12-23 months who have received BCG (%)	78.1	86.9	75.1	64.7	80.9	88.8	96.5	71.6	62.2
15c. Children 12-23 months who have received 3 doses of polio vaccine (%)	78.2	83.1	76.5	74.1	75.4	80.4	87.0	62.8	53.5
15d. Children 12-23 months who have received 3 doses of DPT vaccine (%)	55.3	69.1	50.4	36.9	57.3	68.4	83.5	55.1	51.7
15e. Children 12-23 months who have received measles vaccine (%)	58.8	71.8	54.2	41.0	58.7	71.8	86.1	50.7	42.2
16. Children age 12-35 months who received a vitamin A dose in last 6 months (%)	24.9	26.8	24.2	17.9	25.8	30.7	34.4	na	na
Treatment of childhood diseases (children under 3 years)[3]									
17. Children with diarrhoea in the last 2 weeks who received ORS (%)	26.2	32.7	24.0	18.2	19.2	29.8	43.4	26.9	17.8
18. Children with diarrhoea in the last 2 weeks taken to a health facility (%)	61.5	65.4	60.2	56.2	60.5	64.6	70.4	65.3	61.9
19. Children with acute respiratory infection or fever in the last 2 weeks taken to a health facility (%)	70.5	80.1	67.5	65.6	68.4	74.4	78.8	na	na
Child Feeding Practices and Nutritional Status of Children[3, 3]									
20. Children under 3 years breastfed within one hour of birth (%)	23.4	28.9	21.5	15.9	27.7	29.1	33.0	16.0	9.5
21. Children age 0-5 months exclusively breastfed (%)	46.3	40.3	48.3	48.1	55.9	44.3	40.8	na	na
22. Children age 6-9 months receiving solid or semi-solid food and breastmilk (%)	55.8	62.1	53.8	49.1	51.5	58.4	69.6	na	na
23. Children under 3 years who are stunted (%)	44.9	37.4	47.2	53.2	48.4	41.4	26.3	51.0	na
24. Children under 3 years who are wasted (%)	22.9	19.0	24.1	26.8	25.0	20.4	15.1	19.7	na
25. Children under 3 years who are underweight (%)	40.4	30.1	43.7	50.2	45.8	34.9	20.5	42.7	51.5
Nutritional Status of Ever-Married Adults (age 15-49)									
26. Women whose Body Mass Index is below normal (%)	33.0	19.8	38.8	40.9	34.9	28.7	16.2	36.2	na
27. Men whose Body Mass Index is below normal (%)	28.1	17.5	33.1	38.7	34.6	28.8	15.6	na	na
28. Women who are overweight or obese (%)	14.8	28.9	8.6	7.6	12.1	18.7	30.7	10.6	na
29. Men who are overweight or obese (%)	12.1	22.2	7.3	3.9	6.3	10.2	23.6	na	na
Anaemia among Children and Adults									
30. Children age 6-35 months who are anaemic (%)	78.9	72.2	80.9	84.1	78.1	77.0	69.4	74.2	na
31. Ever-married women age 15-49 who are anaemic (%)	56.2	51.5	58.2	60.2	57.9	54.6	46.6	51.8	na
32. Pregnant women age 15-49 who are anaemic (%)	57.9	54.6	59.0	63.0	58.5	56.2	47.4	49.7	na
33. Ever-married men age 15-49 who are anaemic (%)	24.3	17.2	27.7	33.4	28.9	22.6	16.9	na	na
Knowledge of HIV/AIDS among Ever-Married Adults (age 15-49)									
34. Women who have heard of AIDS (%)	57.0	80.7	46.4	30.7	59.1	78.0	96.7	40.3	na
35. Men who have heard of AIDS (%)	80.0	94.2	73.0	50.7	70.3	88.3	98.3	na	na
36. Women who know that consistent condom use can reduce the chances of getting HIV/AIDS (%)	34.7	56.3	25.1	12.5	26.0	47.5	81.0	na	na
37. Men who know that consistent condom use can reduce the chances of getting HIV/AIDS (%)	68.1	85.6	59.5	33.9	53.0	76.0	93.2	na	na
Women's Empowerment									
38. Currently married women who usually participate in household decisions (%)	36.7	45.0	33.0	34.9	35.2	35.9	43.5	na	na
39. Ever-married women who have ever experienced spousal violence (%)	37.2	30.4	40.2	46.4	42.0	32.4	16.3	na	na

na : Not available
[1] Excludes pregnant women.
[2] Based on the last 2 births in the 3 years before the survey to ever-married women.
[3] Based on WHO standard.
[4] For children education refers to mother's education. Children with missing information on the mother's education are not included in the education columns.

Source: http://www.nfhsindia.org/ . National Family Health Survey. India.

10.2. Table 2.

Sex ratio of total population and child population in the age group 0-6, India : 1961-2011

Year	Sex ratio in age Group 0-6 years	Overall sex ratio
1961	976	941
1971	964	930
1981	962	934
1991	945	927
2001	927	933
2011	914	940

Source: Gender Composition of the Population, Census 2011, published on www.educationforallindia.com